Boiled Sweets

HOW THEY USED TO DO IT

Copyright © 2013 Two Magpies Publishing
An imprint of Read Publishing Ltd
Home Farm, 44 Evesham Road, Cookhill, Alcester,
Warwickshire, B49 5LJ

Commissioning Editor Rose Hewlett
Words by Sophie Berry
Design by Zoë Horn Haywood

All Images remain the copyright property of their respective owners, all attributions and copyright licences are referenced at the rear of the book.

This book is copyright and may not be reproduced or copied in any way without the express permission of the publisher in writing.

British Library Cataloguing-in-Publication Data A catalogue record for this book is available from the British Library.

Contents

Foreword	1
Introduction	3
History of Boiled Sweets	7
Story of the Store Cupboard	11
Wartime Rationing	19
Sourcing Your Supplies	23
Equipment	27
Measurements	33
~ Cup Conversions	36
Temperature	37
~ The Drop Test	44
Techniques	45

Contents

Recipes	51
~ Traditional Favourites	53
~ Fruit Sweets	69
~ Rock Candy	77
~ Lollipops	83
~ Seasonal Treats	89
~ Medicinal & Herbal Sweets	97
~ Wartime Treats	105
Don't Try These at Home!	113
Serving Sweets	117
Gifts	121

Foreword

'Knowledge never learned in schools'
                                            Watson, 1891

The simple pleasure of mastering practical household skills has been all but forgotten over the last century. We live in an overly convenient, disposable world in which things arrive pre-packed, ready-wrapped and lacking in any craft, care, or quality.

It's time to reject this attrition of what were once everyday skills, time to get back to basics, time to remember **How They Used To Do It**.

The **How They Used To Do It** series will take you back to the golden age of practical skills; an age where making and mending, cooking and preserving, brewing and bottling, were all done within the home. The series will instruct you in a whole range of traditional skills that have fallen out of use, putting old knowledge into new hands. Using household items, nifty hints and tricks, and a little creativity you will be surprised what you can achieve.

The series has been carefully curated from a wealth of original resources to provide a wonderful blend of social history and practical instruction. The knowledge within these pages has been sourced from rare books, old newspapers and forgotten magazines to inform a whole new generation about **How They Used To Do It**.

Introduction

Introduction

WELCOME TO THE WONDERFUL WORLD OF BOILED SWEET MAKING.

Introduction

With this little book in your hands you can turn even a humble kitchen into a hub of sweet-making activity, happily passing many a rainy afternoon creating mouth-watering boiled sweets. As well as lots of classic recipes this book is filled with sweet-making tips and techniques you can try as soon as you have mastered the basics.

What's more, you don't need lots of equipment or a vast array of ingredients to get started. Pleasingly, most of the equipment you will need to make even the most complicated-looking boiled sweets will be found already tucked away in your cupboards and cutlery drawer.

Introduction

The beauty of making your own boiled sweets is that you can be sure to use the best and purest ingredients. In an age which tends to be increasingly synthetic, knowing exactly what has gone into your lovingly created confectionery is surely an attractive prospect.

Moreover, the result of sweet-making at home is often much thriftier than buying ready-made sweets. By only making what you want, and in quantities you need, there is no waste.

History of Boiled Sweets

History of Boiled Sweets

People have indulged in sweets for hundreds of years. The term 'sweet' derives from the Olde English 'swete' meaning pleasing to the mind and senses. Early recipes from the 1700s used sticky fruits like figs and dates, along with nuts and honey to create confectionary to sate a sweet tooth.

As sugar became cheaper and more readily available during the nineteenth century, boiled sweets became increasingly popular. By the mid-1800s almost 400 sweet factories had opened up in America alone, and the

History of Boiled Sweets

ease in which boiled sweets could be made and stored at home meant a multitude of exciting new boiled sweets started to appear on stoves and in sweet shops alike.

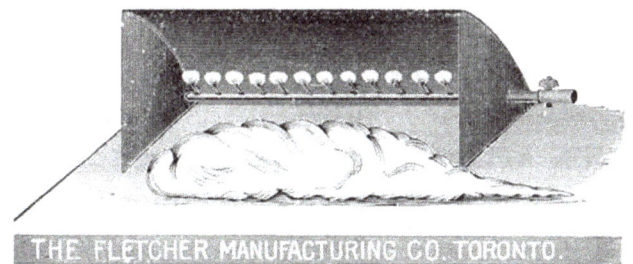

Batch Warmer or Gas Candy Heater.   Price $5.00.

History of Boiled Sweets

The town of Pateley Bridge in Harrogate, North Yorkshire, plays host to the oldest sweet shop in England. The shop, which opened for business in 1827, is the oldest existing sweet shop in the country. It has served generations of sweet-lovers, and still draws a large crowd of visitors every year. The shop still makes boiled sweets using classic recipes, and original equipment. Some of their original copper sweet molds are over one hundred years old.

Story of the Store Cupboard

Story of the Store Cupboard

Kitchens have come an awfully long way in the past century, as have the supplies stocked in pantries and larders. Before modern conveniences such as fridges and freezers, one of the biggest hurdles housewives had to overcome was the task of preserving, and it was no mean feat! It is hard to imagine a world without the convenience of modern kitchen appliances, and keeping food fresh was a daily challenge.

There are many simple preservation methods that can be carried out in the kitchen, without the use of modern conveniences. Salt can be used to cure meat and fish, and pickling can preserve vegetables. The drying of fruit, herbs and spices is especially useful, and can be used across a wide range of recipes including sweets.

Story of the Store Cupboard

Sugar is a natural preservative meaning it could be used by housewives alongside some clever cooking to preserve a glut of seasonal produce or dear fruits, and peels. Jam, chutney, marmalade and confectionery could be made and stockpiled for the coming months.

Having a well-stocked larder was the mark of a good housewife, and before easy preservation and storage methods became common place, boiled sweets would have been a popular addition to the larder's shelves.

Story of the Store Cupboard

STAPLE INGREDIENTS

Now, let's take a little time to get to know the ingredients you will need to make boiled sweets at home. Much like with your kitchen equipment, making sure you have the right supplies is very important before you get started.

You'll be very familiar with most of the ingredients listed in this book, but there may be things that are new to you if you've not made boiled sweets at home before.

Here are a few pantry staples, with a little explanation:

Sugar

Sugar is a staple ingredient, and these days, it is available in many forms. Ready-to-use sugar is a luxury which we now may take for granted, but using sugar in a recipe used to be a much more laborious process.

Until the late nineteenth century, sugar came in the form of sugarloaf. Granulated and cubed sugar came a little later so for a long while, if you wanted to use sugar you had to get to grips with a large sugarloaf cone.

Housewives would buy their sugar in tall, conical loaves, and trim off what they needed with special iron sugar-cutters called sugar nips. If a recipe called for fine, granulated sugar, then a little elbow grease and a pestle and mortar would be enthusiastically employed!

Story of the Store Cupboard

Glucose

Glucose is a type of sugar derived from plants. Conveniently, it is sold in powder form and readily available. Glucose is a very useful addition to your boiled sweets as it decomposes much more easily than regular cane sugar, and will prevent your boiled sweet mixture from crystallising. This is very important, as crystallisation can result in your boiled sweets taking on a grainy, gritty texture.

Glucose is available to buy in supermarkets, or in health food shops. It is well worth sourcing this ingredient, as it will crop up in a variety of sweet recipes.

Story of the Store Cupboard

Cream of Tartar

Cream of tartar is a hugely versatile ingredient, which will be an extremely useful addition to your store cupboard. When used in boiled sweets recipes it will stop the sugar syrup crystallising, much like glucose.

Cream of tartar is so very versatile, that you can use it in many other things around the whole house. Indeed, mixed with a little lemon juice or white vinegar it becomes a wonderful cleaner for metals such as brass, aluminium, and copper. Very useful to know, especially if you are using a copper-bottom jam boiler for your boiled sweet making!

Story of the Store Cupboard

Wartime Rationing

Wartime Rationing

During the 1930s, the country's love affair with sugar came under attack. As World War II air raid sirens sounded throughout Britain's cities, a different war was being fought behind closed doors by the country's army of housewives. Trade routes to the UK were targeted during the war, and food supplies quickly dwindled. On 8 January 1940, bacon, butter and sugar were rationed by the government, followed in subsequent months by meat, tea, jam and much more.

Despite being armed with her government-issued ration book containing coupons for all rationed items, the average housewife's weekly shopping basket was suddenly much

Wartime Rationing

lighter than before. Creating tasty and nutritious meals for the family became a real challenge for many.

Sugar became a very precious resource, and a thriving black market quickly sprung up as a result of the strict rationing. With legitimate supplies so very low, mothers had to be increasingly inventive in order to supply their children and husbands with sweet treats.

Wartime Rationing

Many recipes for sweet substitutes were circulated during wartime Britain, with most ingeniously using the natural sugars from fruits and vegetables such as carrots and beetroot. Boiled sweets were a real treat, and rationed to 12oz per month, so anything a clever housewife could magic up in the kitchen was seen to be a real coup.

Sourcing Your Supplies

Sourcing Your Supplies

These days, you are lucky that you can make sure your pantry is stocked with all that you might need. Gone are the days of visiting a host of shops to get what you need. Without the convenience of large supermarkets, it could take a busy housewife the best part of the day to fill her shopping basket with supplies for the week from her local high street.

And with such an array of mod cons in the kitchen these days, storing ingredients and preparing sweets has never been easier. With a good selection of sweet-making basics in your store cupboard you can try

Sourcing Your Supplies

a huge array of recipes, without the bother of having to go out shopping every time you want to get a batch of boiled sweets bubbling on the stove.

Finding the best ingredients before you put your apron on and start cooking is important, as the lovelier your ingredients are, the lovelier your sweets will be. Look at the local produce on offer in your area. it is so often the case that the best things to eat are the things that grow locally, are in season, and haven't travelled a huge distance. Not only do these things taste better than their imported counterparts, but it is far kinder to the environment to use what is nearby.

Sourcing Your Supplies

Perhaps you have a wonderful local greengrocer who can supply you with seasonal fruit, or a brilliant local health food shop where you can stock up on essences and flavours? Use your local suppliers and their expertise, as their knowledge will be rather useful to you while you are still getting to grips with the basics.

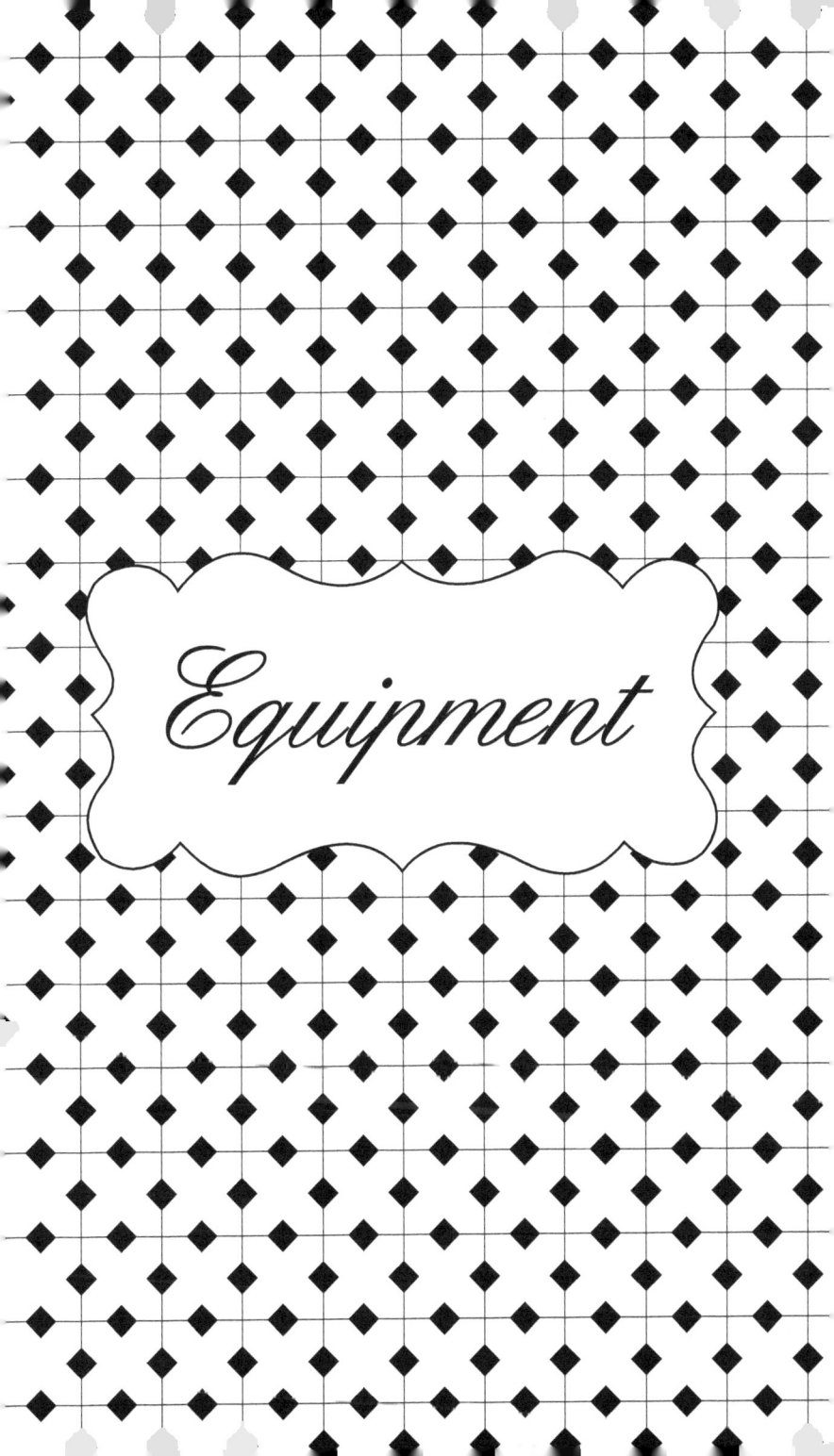

Equipment

Equipment

Now you have stocked your store cupboard, let's have a look at the kitchen equipment you will need to find before getting started on your first batch of boiled sweets . The list of utensils and equipment you will need is not huge, but it is important you have the basics at your fingertips. Your kitchen utensils are the tools of your trade, as it were, and you'll get the best results from your sweet making if you take the time to source the right tools.

Firstly, you will need a large saucepan. A copper-bottomed jam boiler is perfect for this, as it will be designed to withstand very high cooking temperatures, as well as be big

Equipment

enough to contain boiling sugar bubbles. A smaller saucepan will also be necessary, as some recipes require the mixture to be cooked in two batches.

A wooden spoon for stirring the mixture is essential, as plastic may not withstand the high temperature of boiling sugar. As well as this, you will also need a spatula or scraper for working your mixture, and a pair of sharp scissors for snipping your sweets into small pieces. Lightly oil your scissors before use so the sweets don't stick to the scissors, which will make it easier to snip through your ropes of mixture.

Equipment

Many recipes call for you to work the cooling mixture, a technique which we explain a little later in this book. A marble slab, or other heatsafe work surface is best for this. Marble would have been the first port of call for kitchen enthusiasts in the early days of sweet making as it stays nice and cool. A portion of old marble wash stand would make the perfect work surface for boiled sweet making, and you can often find these in second hand shops, or at antique fairs.

Equipment

You may also want to invest in some candy molds and wooden lolly sticks. It is perfectly possible to make boiled sweets without using molds, but many people prefer the quick and easy method of pouring the mixture directly into a mold as opposed to working it by hand. You can also be really creative and make boiled sweets in many different shapes with the use of molds.

Equipment

EQUIPMENT CHECKLIST

LARGE SAUCEPAN

*

SMALL SAUCEPAN

*

MEASURING CUPS AND SCALES

*

SUGAR THERMOMETER

*

WOODEN SPOON

*

BENCH SCRAPER, OR SPATULA

*

SCISSORS

*

SHALLOW BAKING TIN

*

LOLLY STICKS AND MOLDS (OPTIONAL)

*

GREASEPROOF PAPER

Measurements

In the most part, measurements in the recipes in this book will be in cups. A small coffee cup is the best kind to use, and make sure you use the same cup to measure all your ingredients.

You may not be familiar with using cups to measure ingredients but they are a quick and easy way of portioning the rather large quantities of sugar, and other ingredients, some recipes call for.

Cups have been used in cookery for generations, after an American culinary expert called Fanny Farmer introduced them as a standardised form of measurement in recipes. Accuracy and

Measurements

consistency are very important in any recipe, especially for boiled sweets, so Fanny's work was rather groundbreaking at the time.

Fanny published her best-known cookery book 'The Boston Cooking-School Cook Book' in 1896, and it has been used by generations of keen cooks ever since. Fanny introduced these new standardised measurements by stressing the importance of levelling off the cup as you measure. It may seem insignificant, but before her clever intervention, cooks had to make do with instructions such as 'a large dash', 'a goodly pinch', and even 'butter the size of an egg'. Rather amusing, but a little inconsistent, don't you agree?

Measurements

Of course, you don't have to use cups. This table is a handy tool if you need to convert cups into other amounts.

1 cup	8 fluid ounces	½ pint	237 ml
2 cups	16 fluid ounces	1 pint	474 ml
4 cups	32 fluid ounces	1 quart	946 ml
2 pints	32 fluid ounces	1 quart	0.946 l
4 quarts	128 fluid ounces	1 gallon	3.784 l

Temperature

Temperature

Being able to gauge the temperature of your mixture as it cooks is essential when you're making boiled sweets at home. Just a few degrees over or under your desired temperature will result in a very different final product, so it is important that you carefully monitor your boiled sweet mixture as it cooks.

Boiling sugar may seem like quite a demanding task. One must be mindful of safety at all times as it is easy to burn yourself on the cooking mixture. The change in temperature can often be rather rapid so it is very important that you heat the mixture gradually, to avoid a sudden change in temperature.

Temperature

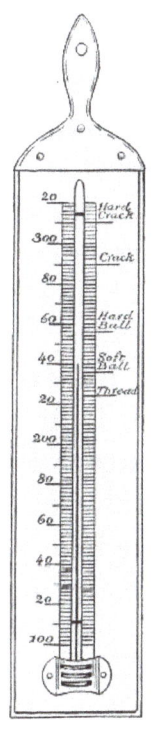

Many of the recipes in this book are classic recipes, which have been used in countless kitchens, by generations of cooks.

The temperatures stated in the recipes in this book will be in Fahrenheit, as this is the original form of measuring temperature. The metric system, which uses the Celsius scale, took some time to be introduced internationally, and Fahrenheit is still widely used to this day.

Temperature

A thermometer is the safest way to monitor the temperature of boiling sugar. It is also the easiest way to gauge the exact temperature of your cooking mixture, so it is a good idea to use one until you have a lot of experience working with boiling sugar.

If you have a new thermometer which hasn't been used before, make sure you break it in. You can do this by placing it into a saucepan of cold water, and then heating the water to boiling point. Remove the pan from the heat, but leave the thermometer in the pan until the water has cooled.

Temperature

Tip

After use, plunge your thermometer into warm water and wipe with a soft cloth.

Remember to do this rather promptly after you have used it, as the boiled sweet mixture will cool, and be very difficult to clean off later.

Temperature

THE DROP TEST

These days we are lucky that sugar thermometers are readily available and are relatively cheap to buy. This was not always the case. Before the introduction of this nifty household tool, another ingenious method had to be employed to test the temperature of boiled sweet mixture as it cooked.

This age old method is called The Drop Test.

By carefully dropping a little mixture into some cold water, you can gauge the stage the mixture is at by the type of mass the mixture forms. Once mastered, this rather ingenious little skill is a failsafe way of monitoring your

Temperature

boiled sweet mixture, and is a truly authentic sweet-making method. If you choose to use the drop test method whilst making your boiled sweets, do be mindful of the dangers of boiling sugar. You don't want a nasty burn, so be very careful when testing your mixture.

Most of the recipes in this book will state to heat the mixture to hard crack stage, which is around 295 to 309°F. If the liquid becomes hard and brittle, and breaks when gently tapped, then you have reached the hard crack stage.

Have a look at the table we have provided for more information on regulating the temperature of your boiled sweet mixture without a thermometer. This should give you a good idea of what to look out for at each stage of cooking.

The Drop Test

Stage	Temperature	Uses
Thread - Forms a thin liquid thread	110°C to 112 °C (230 to 234 °F)	Sugar Syrups
Soft ball - Forms a soft flexible ball that can be flattened.	112°C to 116 °C (234 to 241 °F)	Fudge, pralines, fondant and butter creams
Firm ball - Forms a firm ball that will hold its shape but is still malleable	118°C to 120 °C (244 to 248 °F)	Caramel Candies
Hard ball - Forms thick threads from spoon and creates a hard ball that will hold its shape	121 to 130 °C (250 to 266 °F)	Nougat, marshmallows, gummies, and divinity
Soft crack - Forms firm flexible threads	132°C to 143 °C (270 to 289 °F)	salt water taffy
Hard crack - Forms hard brittle threads that snap easily	146°C to 154 °C (295 to 309 °F)	toffee, brittles, hard candy, and lollipops
Clear liquid - Liquid will begin to change colour. Colour ranges from golden brown to amber	160 °C (320 °F)	caramelised sugar, caramel
Brown liquid - Liquid will begin to change colour. Colour ranges from golden brown to amber	170 °C (338 °F)	caramelised sugar, caramel

Techniques

Techniques

WORKING

Very often boiled sweet recipes will require you to work the cooling mixture. It is a straightforward technique, and is an effective way to blend colouring and flavouring as well as shape your sweets. Some say that working the boiled sweet mixture by hand gives a wonderfully smooth consistency to your final product. Once you have mastered this basic technique you'll be able to make an impressive array of boiled sweets at home in your kitchen.

After you take the saucepan of boiled sweet mixture off the heat, leave the mixture to cool for ten minutes or until a skin forms on the

Techniques

top. Now, it is time to wash your hands, put on an apron, and roll up your sleeves. You'll need a little patience and a spot of elbow grease for this. Wearing a pair of latex gloves will also help protect your hands from the heat.

Once cooled, carefully pour the mixture onto a lightly oiled marble slab or board. A portion of old washstand or work surface is perfect for this, although any heat-safe surface will suffice.

Next, with a bench scraper, begin folding the mixture onto itself repeatedly, working it into the required shape. Keep scraping and folding, especially if you are blending colouring or flavouring into your mixture at this stage. Have a little patience, and repeat this process until the mixture starts to hold its shape.

Techniques

PULLING

Pulling is another technique you should take some time to master. Many of these original recipes will require you to pull the cooling mixture to change the colour of your sweets, and allow you to mold them into the shape. After pulling, your boiled sweets will take on a lovely pearlescent quality, which is not only pretty, but also the sign that you have pulled enough.

The method is important, as the firm pulls completely change the texture of your boiled sweets. Before pulling, the boiled sweet mixture will be a fairly dense mass of sugar. Pulling drags the mixture apart, meaning your sweets won't be too heavy and hard.

Techniques

Here is a straightforward guide to this age old skill.

Once you are happy that you have worked your boiled sweet mixture thoroughly, roll the mixture into a long rope, using your scraper if it is still rather hot. When it is cool enough to handle pull the rope of mixture, stretching it between your hands. Fold the mixture back on itself, twist it together and pull firmly.

Techniques

When your mixture starts taking on a pearly, translucent appearance you know you have pulled enough. A light dusting of icing sugar will stop your hands getting sticky while handling the mixture. Use sharp oiled scissors to snip the long rope into little pieces.

Now, you can take a well-earned rest.

Traditional Favourites

The first batch of recipes we have put together for you to try out are all traditional sweet shop favourites. Perhaps you remember these from your favourite childhood sweet shops, filling jars and stacked high on shelves. Boiled sweets are so wonderfully evocative. A little paper bag filled with your favourites can transport you back to childhood in an instant. What better reason to pick a recipe, and get your first batch of boiled sweets bubbling away.

Acid Drops

This classic recipe for acid drops is the perfect place to start if you are a sweet-making novice. This straightforward recipe can be used as a base for any flavours and colouring, so once you have mastered this you can really get creative with your own variations.

Acid Drops

1 lb sugar
1 cup water
½ oz tartaric acid

1. In a heavy-bottomed saucepan, boil together the water and sugar over a low heat for half an hour. Skim any scum which forms on the surface. **2.** Heat the mixture until hard crack stage, or until the thermometer reads 295°F. **3.** Remove the pan from the heat. Allow the mixture to stand for 5 minutes, or until a skin forms on the surface. **4.** Carefully pour the mixture onto a lightly oiled board or marble slab and add the tartaric acid by dropping it onto the mixture, and working the mixture with a scraper. **5.** As soon as the mixture starts to harden cut it into long strips, roll lengthways and cut into cushions with sharp scissors.

Peppermint Bull's Eyes

Peppermint works fabulously as a flavour in boiled sweets, and is used in many a classic recipe. Adding the refreshing flavour of peppermint to your sweets makes them a perfect after-dinner treat to offer guests at the end of supper, especially as peppermint is a natural digestive aid. Try this classic recipe for peppermint bull's eyes.

Peppermint Bull's Eyes

2 lb brown sugar
½ lb glucose
2 cups water
¼ tsp of peppermint flavouring
2 lb white sugar
1 tsp cream of tartar
2 cups water

---

1. In a heavy-bottomed saucepan boil the brown sugar with 2 cups of water and ½ lb of glucose. **2.** Heat the mixture until hard crack stage, or until the thermometer reads 295°F, and then remove the pan from the heat. **3.** Allow the mixture to stand for 5 minutes, or until a skin forms on the surface. **4.** Carefully pour the mixture onto a lightly oiled board or marble slab. Add the peppermint and work it into the mixture by folding the edges over into the middle. Roll out so it is smooth and flat. **5.** In a smaller pan, repeat steps 1-3, but with the white sugar and cream of tartar. **6.** Work the mixture into a long rope as it cools. Again, take care as the mixture will be hot. **7.** Pull the mixture until it is pearly and translucent. **8.** Wrap the pulled mixture in the peppermint-flavoured mixture, ensuring the whole rope is covered. **9.** Snip small pieces off the long rope, roll into balls and store somewhere airtight and cool.

Barley Sugar

Barley sugar sweets are a truly classic confectionary which were first made back in the seventeenth century. Barley sugar sweets are remembered by many and still found in sweet shops across the country. These subtly flavoured boiled sweets are surprisingly easy to make. Try this recipe for barley sugar - you can add more lemon flavouring if you prefer a slightly sharper taste.

Barley Sugar

½ lb sugar
½ cup water
¼ tsp of lemon essence
¼ tsp of saffron colouring

1. In a heavy-bottomed saucepan, dissolve the sugar in the water. Remove any scum from the surface. **2.** Heat the mixture until hard crack stage, or until the thermometer reads 295°F, and then remove the pan from the heat. **3.** Drop the flavour and colouring into the mixture. Allow the mixture to stand for 5 minutes, or until a skin forms on the surface. **4.** Carefully pour the mixture onto a slab. Work the mixture for a few minutes and smooth it out flat. **5.** Cut into thin strips before it cools, twist these into spirals and leave to harden. **6.** Store somewhere cool and airtight.

Cream Candy

This recipe for cream candy was first published back in 1900, in a book called the 'Home Comforts Range Cook Book'. Unusually, this recipe includes butter which will give your boiled sweets a distinctively creamy, buttery taste.

Cream Candy

2 lb sugar
½ pint water
¼ pint vinegar
1 tbsp butter
1 tsp lemon juice

1. In a heavy-bottomed saucepan, heat the sugar, water, vinegar, lemon juice and butter for fifteen minutes, stirring regularly. **2.** Remove the pan from the heat. **3.** Allow the mixture to stand for 5 minutes, or until a skin forms on the surface. **4.** Carefully pour half of the mixture onto a lightly oiled board or marble slab. **5.** Work the mixture into a long rope and when cool enough to handle, pull until translucent and pearly. **6.** Snip into small pieces, and store in an airtight container.

Molasses Candy

Molasses is an ingredient often found in recipes for boiled sweets. Molasses, if you are not familiar with this sticky, syrupy substance, is the by-product of the sugar refining process. This simple and straightforward recipe for molasses candy was first published in a book called 'The Home Comfort Range Cook Book', circa 1900.

Molasses Candy

---

1 cup molasses
1 tsp bicarbonate of soda

---

1. Boil the molasses in a heavy-bottomed saucepan. **2.** Heat the mixture until hard crack stage, or until the thermometer reads 295°F, and then add the bicarbonate of soda. **3.** Remove the pan from the heat. **4.** Allow the mixture to stand for 5 minutes, or until a skin forms on the surface. **5.** Carefully pour the mixture onto a lightly oiled board, or marble slab **6.** Work the mixture for a few minutes and then shape it into a long rope. **7.** With lightly oiled scissors, snip the rope into small pieces before it cools. **8.** Store somewhere cool and airtight.

Peanut Candy

Nuts are a great addition to boiled sweets, adding a distinctive flavour and satisfying crunch. Try this unusual recipe for peanut candy, which was first featured in a wonderful vintage recipe book called 'The Candy Maker's Guide', back in 1896. This would have been a rather fashionable and cutting edge recipe in its day. The first batches were made in America from recipes dated 1892, and the word 'brittle' was coined around this time too, to describe the distinctively crunchy, nutty sweet.

Peanut Candy

2 oz molasses
1 lb glucose
1 cup water
2 cups peanuts

1. In a heavy-bottomed saucepan, mix the molasses, glucose and water. Heat until the sugar has dissolved.
2. Continue to boil until the mixture reaches 275°F on a sugar thermometer then remove from the heat.
3. Chop the nuts (you can use nuts other than peanuts in this recipe) and put them into a tray. **4.** Carefully pour the mixture over the chopped nuts. **5.** Mark into squares when cool.

Honey Twists

Honey works brilliantly as a flavour in boiled sweets, and is a highly useful ingredient to stock in your store cupboard. Honey has long been associated with sweets and confectionery, from very early treats which consisted of fruit and nuts bound in honey, and later as an alternative to corn syrup in many boiled sweets recipes. Here's a wonderful recipe for honey twists you could try. A little honey essence in a regular boiled sweet mixture is a great way to get a hint of the distinctive flavour.

Honey Twists

½ lb sugar
½ cup water
¼ tsp of honey essence
¼ tsp of saffron colouring

1. In a heavy-bottomed saucepan, dissolve the sugar in the water. Remove any scum from the surface. **2.** Heat the mixture until hard crack stage, or until the thermometer reads 295°F, and then remove the pan from the heat. **3.** Drop the flavour and colouring into the mixture. **4.** Allow the mixture to stand for 5 minutes, or until a skin forms on the surface. **5.** Carefully pour the mixture onto a slab. Work the mixture for a few minutes and smooth it out flat. **6.** Cut into thin strips before it cools, twist these into spirals and leave to harden. **7.** Store somewhere cool and airtight.

Fruit Sweets

The natural sweetness of fruit has been used to create sticky treats for hundreds of years. The very earliest sweet recipes recorded included fruit such as dates and figs, harnessing their natural sweetness, meaning there was no need for sugar at all.

As sugar became cheaper and sweet making really took off, fruit flavours were an obvious addition to the new array of confectionary, giving boiled sweets a delicious fruity tang as well as a lovely jewel-like colour. Below is a selection of some of the best fruity boiled sweets recipes for you to try at home. Once you have mastered the basics, you can experiment with all kinds of different fruit flavours. The possibilities are endless!

Raspberry Candy

Pleasingly, a store cupboard staple can be used to make boiled sweets with much success. Jam can be used in place of food colouring to add a distinctively fruity flavour to your boiled sweets, while also giving your sweet mixture an instant injection of colour. Try this recipe for raspberry candy which uses raspberry jam.

Raspberry Candy

1 lb white sugar
¼ lb raspberry jam
½ cup water
¼ tsp of red or pink colouring (optional)

1. In a heavy-bottomed saucepan, boil the sugar and water until hard crack stage, or until the thermometer reads 295°F. **2.** Add the raspberry jam and stir well. **3.** Remove the pan from the heat and add the colouring. **4.** With a spatula, rub a little mixture against the side of pan until it change and appears opaque. **5.** Carefully pour the mixture into a shallow baking tin lined with greaseproof paper. **6.** Mark into bars with a sharp knife, and break when fully cooled.

Orange Sweets

Citrus fruits work well in boiled sweets recipes as the sharp tang cuts through the sweetness, and gives your sweets an unmistakably zingy flavour. This recipe for orange sweets could easily be adapted if you wish to use a different citrus fruit.

Orange Sweets

3 cups caster sugar
2 ¼ cups golden syrup
1 cup water
1 tbsp orange extract
1 tbsp orange zest, finely grated
½ tsp orange colouring
2 tbsp icing sugar for dusting

1. In a heavy-bottomed saucepan, stir together the sugar, syrup and water. Bring to the boil once the sugar has dissolved. **2.** Heat the mixture until hard crack stage, or until the thermometer reads 295°F, and then remove the pan from the heat. **3.** Stir in colouring and flavouring, and zest if you are using. Carefully pour the mixture onto lightly greased baking trays and dust the top with icing sugar. **4.** Mark into bars when cold, and break when cooled fully. **5.** Store your sweets in an airtight container.

Pear Drops

Pear drops are another fruity boiled sweet that are beloved by many. You can take a trip down memory lane and make your very own pear drops at home with this straightforward recipe. You will need to invest in pear drop molds, but these nifty and inexpensive utensils can be used many times and will really simplify your sweet making.

Pear Drops

4 cups sugar
1 cup glucose
3 cups water
1 tsp tartaric acid
¼ tsp of red food colouring
¼ tsp of yellow food colouring
½ tsp of pear essence

1. In a heavy-bottomed saucepan, dissolve the sugar in the water and add the glucose. **2.** Heat the mixture until hard crack stage, or until the thermometer reads 295°F, and then remove the pan from the heat. **3.** Carefully pour half of the mixture into another heat-safe bowl or saucepan. **4.** Add red colouring to one batch and yellow to another. **5.** Carefully spoon your mixture into pear drop molds. Half fill the mold with one colour and top up with the other colour. **6.** Turn out when cool and store somewhere dry and cool.

Rock Candy

Rock candy is a term found in many confectionary recipe books and can refer to a few kinds of sweets. It can be used to describe the chunky sticks of pulled candy so beloved of visitors to seaside resorts. These fun souvenirs often have writing running through the length of the stick, and come in an array of bright colours.

Others may know rock candy as a type of crystallised, non-pulled confectionary. You might find this kind of rock candy on a rope, or on a stick. This type of crystallised candy looks like little pebbles or gems, perhaps hence the name.

Edinburgh Rock

Edinburgh rock is a traditional Scottish sweet and is another variant of rock candy. It was first made in the 19th Century by a man named Alexander Ferguson, who became known as 'Sweetie Sandy'. He learned the confectionery trade in Glasgow, and then moved to Edinburgh to set up his own business. There are many variations of rock, but this much-loved recipe for the Edinburgh variety is a perfect place to start.

Edinburgh Rock

1 lb granulated sugar
1 ½ cups water
½ tsp cream of tartar
¼ tsp of cinnamon essence
¼ tsp of rose essence
¼ tsp of red colouring

1. In a heavy-bottomed saucepan, dissolve the sugar in the water. Add the cream of tartar. **2.** Heat the mixture until hard crack stage, or until the thermometer reads 295°F, and then remove the pan from the heat. **3.** Allow the mixture to stand for 5 minutes, or until a skin forms on the surface. **4.** Carefully pour half of the mixture into a flat oiled tin. Add the colouring and rose essence and work the mixture with a scraper, folding the sides over to the centre to blend. **5.** As the first batch cools, repeat this process with the other half of the mixture, but this time using cinnamon. **6.** When both batches are cool enough to handle, work them into long ropes and pull until they are pearly and translucent. **7.** Twist the two long lengths of Edinburgh rock together and then snip them into little pieces with sharp, oiled scissors. Store your sweets somewhere cool and airtight.

Almond Rock

Here's another great little recipe for rock candy. This one uses almonds, which have been a key ingredient in sweets since the very earliest confections of the middle ages. Almonds also have a number of health benefits, and will help keep your hair and skin in good condition.

Almond Rock

2 ½ lb brown sugar
½ lb glucose
1 ½ lb pounds sweet almonds
3 cups of water
¼ tsp lemon essence

1. In a heavy-bottomed saucepan, heat the sugar and glucose in the water. **2.** Heat the mixture until hard crack stage, or until the thermometer reads 295°F, and then remove the pan from the heat. **3.** Allow the mixture to stand for 5 minutes, or until a skin forms on the surface. **4.** Carefully pour the mixture onto a lightly oiled board or marble slab. **5.** Drop the essence onto the mixture, and sprinkle the nuts onto the mixture. **6.** Work the mixture with a scraper, folding the sides over to the centre to blend. **7.** When the almonds are well blended, work the mixture into a long rope and with a sharp knife, cut the rope into small pieces. **8.** Store your sweets somewhere cool and airtight.

Lollipops

Lollipops are great fun, and very easy to make. The origin of the name itself is also rather interesting. The word made its way into the English language towards the end of the eighteenth century, and used the slang term for mouth, 'lolly' which was popular at this time. So, by very definition, lollipops are simply something that you pop in your mouth.

Interestingly, early lollies didn't actually have a stick to hold. This came later, during the twentieth century when lollipops became popular with children and sweet-makers found the addition of a stick to grasp stopped little fingers from becoming sticky!

You can easily make lollies at home without molds, so don't be put off if you are yet to invest in these. You simply need some wooden lolly sticks, although you will find chopsticks to be a perfectly serviceable substitution.

Lollipops

Here's a great basic recipe for lollipops to get you started. Get creative and see which flavours work best. The sky's the limit with these sweet treats, and you can flavour them with just about anything.

Lollipops

1 lb granulated sugar
1 cup water
½ tsp cream of tartar
¼ tsp of flavouring and colouring - anything you like!

---

1. In a heavy-bottomed saucepan, dissolve the sugar in the water over a low heat. **2.** Boil your mixture steadily until hard crack stage, or until the thermometer reads 295°F, and then remove the pan from the heat. **3.** Allow your mixture to cool for a few minutes in the saucepan then carefully spoon out small amounts onto a marble slab, or other smooth work surface. Greaseproof paper also works well. **4.** Using a scraper, work these blobs of mixture into lollipop shapes and insert a wooden stick into each. Leave to set hard.

Liqueur Lollies

And now, here's something for the grown ups. Adding liqueur to your boiled sweets is very easy and straightforward, and is a great way to craft a treat for adults. Liqueur was first added to boiled sweets in the late 1930s by a confectioner from Kentucky named **Ruth Hanly Booe**. She championed the use of bourbon in boiled sweets, but it is worth noting that tequila works particularly well, too.

If you would prefer to make these as drops and not lollies, simply spoon a little mixture onto a sheet of baking paper to make the individual drops, and leave them to cool.

Liqueur Lollies

¾ cup icing sugar
¼ cup bourbon
3 tbsp golden syrup
2 tbsp cold water
¼ tsp of red colouring
A pinch of salt

1. Put the liqueur into a heavy-bottomed saucepan, leaving a few teaspoons for later. **2.** Add the water, sugar, salt and syrup to the saucepan. **3.** Heat the mixture on a medium heat and bring to the boil. Stir until the sugar dissolves, then let the mixture boil for five minutes without stirring it. **4.** Remove the pan from the heat. Add the rest of the liqueur to the mixture, along with any colouring you are using. Stir the mixture well. **5.** Carefully pour the mixture into lollipop molds, or spoon onto greaseproof paper if you are not using molds. Insert the lolly sticks. **6.** Once cool, dust the lollies in a little icing sugar and store an airtight container.

Seasonal Treats

Boiled sweets can be enjoyed all year round. No excuse is needed to get a batch of your favourite treats on the stove in our humble opinion.

However, there are certain times of the year that lend themselves rather well to sweet making, and certain recipes go hand-in-hand with seasonal celebrations. Valentine's day, Easter, Bonfire Night, and of course Christmas.

As well as being a real treat to have stocked at home, boiled sweets make perfect gifts for all manner of occasions. A lovingly created batch of sweets, carefully wrapped and packaged, is a thoughtful gift, and you can make large batches with ease and relative thriftiness.

Rosebuds

This rather lovely recipe for Rosebuds is the perfect boiled sweet to make to celebrate St. Valentine's day. This recipe was first printed in 'The Candy Maker's Guide', an early confectionery recipe book which was published in 1896.

Rosebuds

2 pounds white sugar
½ pounds glucose
½ tsp rose water
⅔ pint water
½ tsp red food colouring

1. In a heavy-bottomed saucepan heat the sugar, glucose and water until it reaches 300°F, or until the mixture forms a hard, brittle mass when tested in cold water. **2.** Remove the pan from the heat, and carefully pour it onto a marble slab or lightly oiled board. **3.** Set aside one third of the mixture for pulling, and add the red food colouring and rose water to the larger portion of mixture. **4.** Pull the smaller piece of mixture until pearly and white in colour. **5.** Spread out the larger piece on your work surface and lay the pulled sugar in the middle. **6.** Carefully wrap the red mixture around the pulled candy, and snip into small pieces.

Toffee Apples

Toffee apples are great fun to make, and so very nostalgic. Surely we must all remember the excitement of unwrapping a huge, sticky apple on bonfire night and crunching through the sweet toffee.

A candy maker from Newark in America is said to be the first person to make toffee apples.

William Kolb made his first batch of toffee apples to sell at Christmas during the winter of 1908. He sold them for 5 cents a piece, and soon toffee apples were being produced across America.

Coating fruit in sticky syrup like this dates back even further than the first toffee apples of the nineteenth century. This method has been used for hundreds of years as a way of preserving fruit, as well as turning it into a decadent sweet treat. Try this fantastic recipe for toffee apples.

Toffee Apples

2 cups granulated sugar
½ cup white vinegar
½ cup water
1 tsp golden syrup
A drop of colouring / flavouring (optional)
10 apples

1. Insert lolly sticks into your apples and put them to one side. **2.** In a heavy bottomed saucepan, heat the sugar and water for 5 mins. Add the vinegar, then stir in the golden syrup. **3.** Heat the mixture until hard crack stage, or until the thermometer reads 295°F, and then remove the pan from the heat. **4.** Add flavourings or colouring if you are using them. **5.** Carefully roll each apple in the mixture then lay onto baking parchment to cool. **6.** Repeat. Wrap your toffee apples in greaseproof paper or cellophane to stop them getting sticky.

Tip: When you're making toffee apples, avoid using particularly glossy apples or fruit that has been waxed. Although these apples look beautiful in a fruit bowl, it will very difficult for the toffee mixture to bond with such a smooth surface. Golden Delicious, or russet apples work well, as their skins tend to be more textured.

Candy Canes

Christmas is the perfect time to get busy in the kitchen and really put your boiled sweet-making skills to the test. There is something extra special about a present which has been handmade, and boiled sweets make a great gift for children and adults alike. Why not try this recipe for festively striped peppermint candy canes? They can even be used to decorate your Christmas tree.

Candy Canes

3 cups sugar
5 tbsp liquid glucose
2 cups water
½ teaspoon cream of tartar
½ teaspoon peppermint oil

---

1. In a heavy-bottomed saucepan, mix the sugar and glucose and add the water. Heat until the sugar has dissolved. **2.** Add the cream of tartar, and bring the mixture to the boil. **3.** Continue to boil until the mixture reaches 275 °F on a sugar thermometer. **4.** Remove the pan from the heat and add the peppermint oil. **5.** Carefully pour the mixture into candy cane molds. **6.** Using a little red food colouring, paint stripes onto your candy canes when they are set.

Medicinal & Herbal Sweets

For hundreds of years, people have turned to the naturally healing powers of herbs to treat coughs, colds and congestion. Other natural ingredients such a peppermint and lemon have also been used to treat a range of ailments, including nausea, and digestion problems. However, it wasn't until boiled sweets grew in popularity during the nineteenth century that these remedies were incorporated into a sweet, and the cough drop was first created.

One of the first mass-produced cough drops was the Smith Brothers cough drop. James Smith was a restaurateur who was introduced to a cough drop recipe, and decided to make a batch in his kitchen. The cough drops were a success, and he began selling them in large quantities.

Smith's sons took over the thriving business after his death, and the fledgeling company continued to go from strength to strength.

You too can create natural cough drops at home, with a handful of easy-to-find ingredients.

Herbal Cough Drops

You can easily make your own cough drops at home, and they really are the perfect thing to soothe a nasty head cold or scratchy sore throat. Try adding a few drops of eucalyptus or other natural anti-decongestants such as menthol to your boiled sweet recipes for the perfect natural remedy.

Herbal Cough Drops

1 lb sugar
½ lb glucose syrup
½ cup water
¼ tsp of eucalyptus oil

1. In a heavy-bottomed saucepan, heat the sugar, syrup and water until hard crack stage, or until the thermometer reads 295°F **2.** Remove the pan from the heat and add the eucalyptus oil. Stir well. **3.** Carefully place drops of mixture onto a lightly oiled board or marble slab with a teaspoon. **4.** Remove the drops when they are cool.

Horehound, Honey & Menthol Cough Drops

Horehound is a natural cough suppressant, and when added to a boiled sweet recipe along with other ingredients such a menthol and peppermint, can be a really effective remedy in fighting coughs, colds and painful congestion.

Try this simple recipe for horehound cough drops.

Horehound, Honey & Menthol Cough Drops

1 lb sugar
2 oz honey
4 oz glucose
4 oz horehound
1 tsp menthol
1 tbsp starch
Water to cover

1. In a heavy-bottomed saucepan heat the sugar, water, glucose and horehound and until the thermometer reads 300ºF, or the mixture forms brittle threads when tested in cold water. **2.** Add the honey, and stir well. **3.** Remove the pan from the heat, and allow it to cool for ten minutes, or until a skin has formed on the surface. **4.** Carefully pour the mixture onto a lightly oiled board or other smooth surface, and drop the menthol and starch onto the mixture. **5.** Work the mixture by folding the edges over to the centre repeatedly, and kneading well. **6.** Roll the mixture into a long rope, and snip into small pieces with a pair of sharp, oiled scissors.

Brown Cough Drops

Another useful addition to your store cupboard, which may well be in there already, are cloves. Cloves have strong antiseptic, anti-inflammatory and antioxidant properties. This fantastic recipe for cough drops harnesses the powers of cloves, aniseed and our other medicinal favourite - horehound.

Brown Cough Drops

**1 ¾ lb brown sugar
4 oz glucose
2 tsp tartaric acid
½ tsp aniseed oil
¼ tsp clove oil
¼ tsp peppermint oil
1 tsp horehound
2 cups water**

1. In a heavy-bottomed saucepan, boil the horehound in water for ten minutes, and then strain it. **2.** To this water, add the sugar and glucose and boil First boil the herb horehound in the water ten minutes, then strain; add the liquor to the sugar and the glucose, and boil until the thermometer reads 310ºF, or the mixture forms brittle threads when tested in cold water. **3.** Remove the pan from the heat, and allow it to cool for ten minutes, or until a skin forms on the surface. **4.** Carefully pour the mixture onto a lightly oiled board or other heat-safe surface. **5.** Drop the tartaric acid onto the mixture, and add the aniseed, clove and peppermint. **6.** Work the mixture by folding the edges over to the centre repeatedly, and kneading well. **7.** Roll the mixture into a long rope, and snip into small pieces with a pair of sharp, oiled scissors.

Wartime Treats

During strict wartime rationing in Great Britain, housewives had to get creative to make their rather meagre supplies stretch. Any recipe which didn't use sugar was rather precious, as sugar was incredibly scarce. The next selection of recipes uses a range of sugar substitutes, including honey, sticky fruits and even potato, which would have been invaluable during the rationing era.

Tutti Frutti Bites

These tutti frutti bites are an unusual sweet treat which uses no sugar at all. Sticky fruits like figs and dates have been used to make confectionery since the 1700s, and are still popular additions to this day. You can use a mixture of your favourite fruit for this, and a dash of your favourite liqueur makes these little bites a truly indulgent treat.

Tutti Frutti Bites

1 cup figs
1 cup seedless raisins
1 cup pitted dates
1 tbsp candied citron
2 tbsp liqueur
½ cup chopped nuts
1 tbsp icing sugar, for dusting

1. Steam the fruits and nuts until they are soft and tender. **2.** Chop the steamed fruits very finely, adding a little brandy as you go. You could use a food processor for this if you prefer. **3.** Mold the mixture into bite-sized chunks, and chill in the fridge for 2-4 hours. **4.** Dust with icing sugar, and store them somewhere cool and dry.

Honey Drops

You can even use honey as a single ingredient, as shown in this nifty little honey drop recipe. This recipe would have been very valuable during wartime sugar rationing, and is still incredibly useful today. This is the great way to create boiled sweets without the large quantities of sugar most recipes use, making them a perfect treat for little children.

Honey Drops

½ cup honey

1. In a heavy-bottomed saucepan, heat the honey until hard crack stage, or until the thermometer reads 295°F. **2.** Remove the pan from the heat. Stir well. **3.** Carefully place drops of mixture onto a lightly oiled board, or marble slab with a teaspoon. **4.** Remove the drops when they are cool.

Potato Coconut Candy

The abundance of potatoes in Europe, and later in America paved the way for some very unusual sounding sweet recipes. Recipes which creatively use potatoes are found in a host of cookbooks from the nineteenth century, and came to be invaluable during the strict sugar wartime rationing.

Here's a fabulously unusual recipe for potato coconut candy for you to try. This recipe was first published in the 1920s in the popular recipe book, 'Rigby's Reliable Candy Teacher'.

Potato Coconut Candy

1 medium sized potato
2 cups sugar
2 cups shredded coconut
1 tsp vanilla
2 oz chocolate

1. Boil or bake the potato until well done, and then push it through a coarse sieve or a potato ricer. There should be half a cup of potato. **2.** Melt the chocolate in a bowl over warm water. **3.** Add the sugar, coconut, and vanilla to the potato, working together until well mixed. **4.** Press the mixture into a small baking tin and spread the top with the chocolate. **5.** When the chocolate has cooled and set, cut into small pieces and store somewhere cool.

Don't Try These at Home!

Don't Try These at Home!

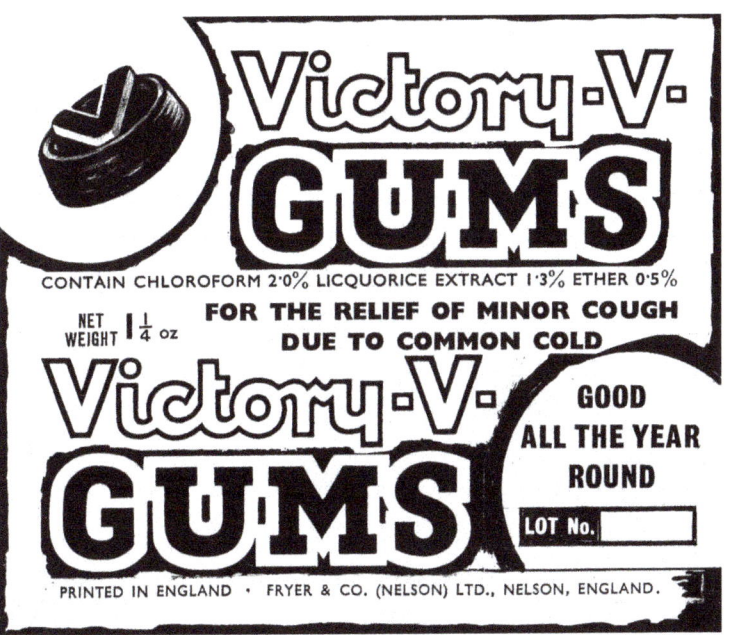

Don't Try These at Home!

Over the years, there has been an array of rather questionable confectionary on the market. Many ingredients which are now illegal, such as opium, cannabis and cocaine were once found merrily medicating the masses in a range of innocuous sounding sweets, such as cocaine tooth drops. Adding to this, some of the natural ingredients recommended in recipes for medicinal sweets from times gone by are rather unpalatable, to say the least.

The following sweets are just a few of the weird and wonderful confections that have been crafted over the years. We must stress that you shouldn't attempt to recreate them at home.

Don't Try These at Home!

Army and Navy sweets were a strongly-flavoured sweet, similar in taste to cough sweets. Traditionally they were used by troops for their medicinal qualities, and by civilians during winter to ward off coughs and colds. Originally, the sweets' ingredients list included camphorated tincture of opium, although this was later removed.

Victory V was a British brand of liquorice-flavoured lozenges which were made in Lancashire in the mid nineteenth century, and eventually mass produced throughout Great Britain. Controversially, the sweets originally contained chloroform, ether, and even cannabis. The sweets are still available today, although their recipe has changed somewhat.

Don't Try These at Home!

Pine tar is a natural product of pine trees, and has many medicinal uses. As a highly effective natural anti-septic, pine tar was a useful addition to cough drops, helping fight infections of the mouth and throat which cause pain. However, it has to be said that the strong flavour was not to everyone's taste.

Another traditional cough remedy is Iceland Moss, so named as it was first found on lava slopes in Iceland. Iceland Moss is also found on the mountains of north Wales, north England, Scotland and Ireland. Despite it's rather unappealing sounding name, Iceland Moss is said to be a very effective remedy, and when masked with other ingredients, the mossy taste is barely discernable.

Serving Sweets

Serving Sweets

Finding new and interesting recipes to impress dinner party guests could be a daunting prospect for a hostess, but offering carefully crafted homemade sweets to guests at the end of the evening was seen to be an elegant touch. Traditionally, boiled sweets would have been served at the end of supper, perhaps to accompany coffee. A selection of sweets were placed in a pretty dish and offered to guests. A classic recipe containing

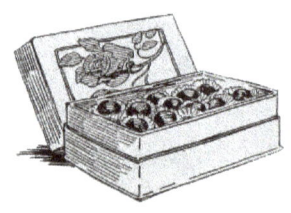

Serving Sweets

peppermint would have made a very dainty alternative to an after-dinner mint after a heavy meal.

Today, you can still find beautiful antique glass and china dishes specifically for serving sweets. Some have lids but some are made without lids and are perfect for serving your sweets to guests at the dinner table.

Serving Sweets

Display your sweets in vintage glass or recycled jars and place them around the house as both decorations and tempting treats.

Gifts

There is nothing nicer than a handmade gift, and what better way to make the most of your new-found sweet-making skills than to give it to a loved one as a present. Homemade boiled sweets make the perfect Christmas or birthday gift, and you can even add your loved ones' favourite ingredients to the recipe for a truly personal touch.

Gifts

Fold your sweets into greaseproof paper or cellophane to make sure they don't stick together and carefully wrap your gift. Small cardboard boxes from craft shops are also perfect this, and can be wrapped in festive paper, too.

We hope you have enjoyed this little book about the wonderful world of making boiled sweets. We hope we have we have been able to provide a wealth of useful and practical information that can be passed on again, so that these invaluable skills will not be lost.

Credits and Attributions

Cover Image, Title page and Page 4 - This work is a derivative of "1956-Electrolux" is copyright © October 17, 2009 James Vaughn, x-ray delta one, made available on Flickr under Creative Commons Attribution 2.0 Generic (CC BY 2.0) http://www.flickr.com/photos/x-ray_delta_one/4017899831/sizes/l/in/faves-90808113@N04/

Page 9 - This work is a derivative of "Pg.76, Batch Warmer or Gas Candy Heater. Price $5.00." is Copyright © 1896, The Candy Maker's Guide, by Fletcher Manufacturing Company made available on Gutenburg under The Public Domain Licence http://www.gutenberg.org/files/30293/30293-h/30293-h.htm

Page 13 - This work is a derivative of "Waste Not want not" is Copyright © 1914 Canadian Food Board, Hamilton [Ontario, Canada] : Howell Lith., made available onwww.loc.gov/ under The Public Domain Licence http://www.loc.gov/pictures/item/2005696499/

Page 18 - This work is a derivative of "whenmotherletsus inside page" is Copyright © 1915 New York, Moffat, Yard and company, made available on Archive under The Public Domain Licence http://archive.org/details/whenmotherletsus00bach

Page 21 - This work is a derivative of "Do with less, so they'll have enough! Rationing gives you your fair share" is Copyright © 1943, posted by United States. Office of War Information. Division of Public Inquiries, made available on UNT Digital Library under The Public Domain Licence http://digital.library.unt.edu/ark:/67531/metadc538/?q=Rationing

Page 22 - This work is a derivative of "Your Sugar Ration 1917 - ca. 1919" is Copyright ©1917 U.S. Food Administration. Educational Division. Advertising Section, made available on Wikimedia under The Public Domain Licence http://commons.wikimedia.org/wiki/File:%22This_Store_is_pledged_to_conform_to_the_Sugar_Regulations_of_the_Food_Administration._Your_Sugar_Ration_is_2lbs._per_mo_-_NARA_-_512525.jpg

Page 24 - This work is a derivative of "It's All You Need" is Copyright © 1950 Posted by noluck_boston, made available on vintage-ads.livejournal.com http://vintage-ads.livejournal.com/tag/cleaning

Page 26 - This work is a derivative of "Narragansett Electric Co.'s Fat and Grease – Pass the Ammunition (1943)" is Copyright © 1943 posted by Ginevra, midniterose, made available on vintage-ads.livejournal.com http://vintage-ads.livejournal.com/tag/ww2%20rationing

Page 28 - This work is a derivative of "Pg. 94, COPPER CANDY LADLE. Fig 7" is Copyright © 1896, The Candy Maker's Guide, by Fletcher Manufacturing Company made available on Gutenburg under The Public Domain Licence http://www.gutenberg.org/files/30293/30293-h/30293-h.htm

Page 29 - This work is a derivative of "Pg. 94, COPPER CANDY LADLE. Fig 8" is Copyright © 1896, The Candy Maker's Guide, by Fletcher Manufacturing Company made available on Gutenburg under The Public Domain Licence http://www.gutenberg.org/files/30293/30293-h/30293-h.htm

Page 30 Page 31 Page 32 Page 34 - This work is a derivative of "whenmotherletsus pg 17" is Copyright © 1915 New York, Moffat, Yard and company, made available on Archive under The Public Domain Licence http://archive.org/details/whenmotherletsus00bach

Page 32 - This work is a derivative of "LIFE Dec 12, 1955 hamilton watches christmas spread" is Copyright © 1955, posted by Jocelmeow, made available on vintage-ads.livejournal.com http://vintage-ads.livejournal.com/tag/1945

Page 35 - This work is a derivative of "Maxwell House Coffee (1950) " is Copyright © 1950 posted by, pikkewyntjie made available on vintage-ads.livejournal.com http://vintage-ads.livejournal.com/tag/1950

Page 39 - This work is a derivative of "whenmotherletsus pg 18" is Copyright © 1915 New York, Moffat, Yard and company, made available on Archive under The Public Domain Licence http://archive.org/details/whenmotherletsus00bach

Page 41 - This work is a derivative of "Diced Cream of America Co., 1949" is Copyright © 1949, posted by Man Writing Slash (write_light), made available on vintage-ads.livejournal.com http://vintage-ads.livejournal.com/tag/1949

Page 49 - This work is a derivative of "whenmotherletsus pg 51" is Copyright © 1915 New York, Moffat, Yard and company, made available on Archive under The Public Domain Licence http://archive.org/details/whenmotherletsus00bach

Page 50 - This work is a derivative of "Wright's Coal Tar Soap Ad, Child asleep near mother, 1922" is Copyright © 1922 Wright's Coal Tar Soap made available on wikimedia and flickr under The Public Domain Licence http://commons.wikimedia.org/wiki/File:Wright's_Coal_Tar_Soap,_1922.jpg

Page 113 - This work is a derivative of "Original artwork for litho origination for Victory V Gums cough sweets containing ether, chloroform and licquorice extract." is Copyright © 1920 by Smith & Ritchie, made available on Flickr under The Public Domain Licence http://www.flickr.com/photos/30239838@N04/3817281743/sizes/l/

Page 118 - This work is a derivative of "whenmotherletsus pg 26" is Copyright © 1915 New York, Moffat, Yard and company, made available on Archive under The Public Domain Licence http://archive.org/details/whenmotherletsus00bach

Page 119 - This work is a derivative of "Vintage ChinaTaken from Mrs Beetons Everyday Cookery & Housekeeping" is Copyright © 1893, posted by tiffany terry, libertygrace0 made available on flickr under Creative commons Attribution 2.0 Generic (CC BY 2.0) http://www.flickr.com/photos/35168673@N03/4392797084/in/set-72157627296287304

Page 120 - This work is a derivative of "Three legged glass dish" is Copyright © January 27, 2012 , Joanna Bourne, made available on flickr under Creative commons Attribution 2.0 Generic (CC BY 2.0) http://www.flickr.com/photos/66992990@N00/6773469145/sizes/l/

Page 122 - This work is a derivative of "Tiffany Blue" is Copyright © May 18, 2008, Jill Clardy, made available on flickr under Creative commons Attribution 2.0 Generic (CC BY 2.0) http://www.flickr.com/photos/jillclardy/2523850043/

Page 123 - This work is a derivative of "UH-OH - Oreo / Nabisco, 1951" is Copyright © 1951, posted by Man Writing Slash (write_light), made available on vintage-ads.livejournal.com http://vintage-ads.livejournal.com/tag/1919

www.ingramcontent.com/pod-product-compliance
Lightning Source LLC
Chambersburg PA
CBHW070614170426
43200CB00012B/2692